THE AUTHORITY GUIDE TO
BEHAVIOUR IN
BUSINESS

How to inspire others and build
successful relationships

ROBIN HILLS

The Authority Guide to Behaviour in Business

How to inspire others and build successful relationships

© Robin Hills

ISBN 978-1-912300-08-2
eISBN 978-1-912300-09-9

Published in 2017 by Authority Guides
authorityguides.co.uk

Contents

Experience is not what happens to you –
it's how you interpret what happens to you.

Aldous Huxley

Introduction

Some people are naturally great with other people. However, for most people it takes a dedicated amount of time and energy to build good, powerful business relationships that are authentic and lasting. They are such an integral and necessary part of success, but many people don't seem to want to put in the work. Successful and powerful business relationships just don't happen without dedicated, consistent work.

Being human means that we are all susceptible to making mistakes and errors due to the limitations of our brain. However, within the workplace it is important to recognise how our behaviour drives our interactions with other people and how it affects the relationships that we build with others. Learning from our mistakes and adopting methods to gain insights help to keep us, our colleagues and our clients safe. Understanding how we are fallible can help us to determine what we can do about it.

Understanding how people behave, what motivates them and why they respond in certain ways will help in developing better quality connections with people and allow you to interact with them more authentically. This will ensure that the relationship that develops is more rewarding for everyone.

How this book will help you

This book is crammed with insights and practical tips. It informs you about ways to:

- change the way you think about yourself and how you approach situations
- move forward and build your understanding of working with your behaviour at your own pace
- understand how emotional intelligence and social intelligence can help you to make better decisions and build quality relationships.

There are three ways to read this book:

1. Skim through quickly looking for advice when faced with a particular set of events

2. Read it carefully and, when you've finished it, find out more about the subject

3. Treat the book as a practical manual, and begin applying the tips before you've reached the end

The best approach is the third option. Of course, there's nothing wrong with looking for help with a particular issue or reading around the subject further. If you only do these things, you run the risk of missing out on a lot of extra information about transforming other areas of your life. You might also miss out on developing a great academic understanding about the non-technical skills of human factors, and emotional intelligence and social intelligence without actually changing your behaviour.

Emotional and social intelligence

Effective leaders are distinguished not by their cognitive intelligence (intelligence quotient; IQ) or subject knowledge, but by their emotional and social intelligence. Cognitive intelligence is fixed around the age of 17, whereas both emotional and social intelligence can be developed and improved over time.

Many organisations have leaders with high IQs but who are lacking in emotional and social intelligence. In challenging situations, low levels of these intelligences can manifest themselves as passive, aggressive or passive-aggressive communication skills, bullying, perfectionism, avoidance, denial, procrastination, blame, controlling behaviours, obsessive behaviour, using anger as a shield, refusing to ask for help or not listening to feedback from trusted others.

Emotional and social intelligence helps business leaders to successfully address fundamental challenges in a changing workplace and drive performance. Research has found that individuals with strong leadership potential tend to have higher levels of emotional and social intelligence, suggesting that they are significant qualities for business leaders and managers to have. As the pace of change is increasing and the world of work is making ever greater demands on a person's cognitive, emotional and physical resources, this particular set of abilities is becoming increasingly important.

Emotional and social intelligence at work

To be truly effective within a work context, a person has to learn how to interact with others, and how to negotiate their way through life's events and experiences. These are the realms of social and emotional intelligence.

In the context of the workplace, emotional intelligence includes a person's capacity to recognise and manage their own emotions, and perceive and deal with the feelings of others – either collectively, or on an individual basis.

An emotionally intelligent person has self-awareness and self-control; the ability to communicate, motivate and influence others; and the capability of building bonds and creating group synergies. They also have a greater understanding of their own psychological state – a condition that can extend to effectively managing stressful situations.

Social intelligence considers both situational awareness and meaningful interaction. A socially intelligent person is able to work well with others and understand the dynamics within a group. They are also able to take into consideration how circumstances and environmental factors impact on people at an individual and team level.

Generally speaking, those who effectively combine both intelligences find it easier to build and maintain relationships with other people, and to be a part of group situations. They can have a high degree of self-awareness, which allows them to use their confidence and insight to be a team leader and a team player.

Emotional intelligence as an ability

In 1990, John (Jack) Mayer and Peter Salovey introduced the concept of emotional intelligence suggesting that some individuals possess the ability to reason about and use emotions to enhance thought more effectively than others. Through their research, they suggested that emotional intelligence is a set of four interrelated abilities:

- Perceiving emotions. The ability to detect and decipher emotions in faces, pictures, voices and cultural artefacts – including the ability to identify one's own emotions.
- Using emotions. The ability to use emotions to facilitate cognitive activities, such as thinking and problem solving.
- Understanding emotions. The ability to comprehend the language of emotion and to appreciate complicated relationships among emotions and the way they evolve over time.
- Managing emotions. The ability to regulate emotions in both ourselves and in others.

Emotional intelligence as a series of competencies

The popular understanding of emotional intelligence came about through the publication of Daniel Goleman's (1995) bestselling book, *Emotional Intelligence: Why it can matter more than IQ.*

Goleman identified the five key elements of emotional intelligence as:

- Self-awareness: knowing your emotions
- Self-regulation: managing your own emotions

- Motivation: motivating yourself and others
- Empathy: recognising and understanding other people's emotions
- Social skills: managing relationships through managing the emotions of others (see Figure 1)

Figure 1 The five key elements of emotional intelligence

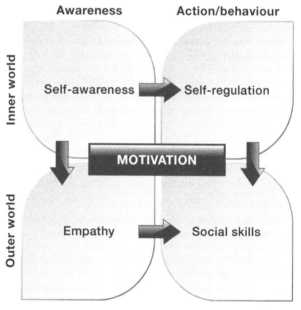

In 1998, Goleman published a follow-up book, *Working with Emotional Intelligence*, linking success in business leadership with emotional intelligence. In the book he describes this success as 'the capacity for recognising our own feelings and those of others, for motivating ourselves, for managing emotions well in ourselves and in our relationships'.

Measuring emotional intelligence

Since the 1990s, there have been many commercial psycho-metric assessments that have become available based on the various models of emotional intelligence.

Ability based

The Mayer-Salovey-Caruso Emotional Intelligence Test (the MSCEIT) is based on a series of emotion-based problem-solving items. Consistent with the authors' claim of emotional intelligence as a type of intelligence, the test is modelled on ability-based IQ tests.

Trait based

Trait emotional intelligence refers to an individual's self-perceptions of their emotional abilities and is investigated within a personality framework using the Trait Emotional Intelligence Questionnaire (TEIQue).

Mixed model (usually combined with trait-based measures)

The Emotional and Social Competency Inventory (ESCI) was developed in 2007 by Daniel Goleman together with Richard Boyatzis. This provides a behavioural measure of emotional and social competencies.

The Emotional Quotient Inventory (EQ-i 2.0) incorporates per-sonality and ability. It is the most widely used assessment glob-ally, and is considered to be the most scientifically valid and reli-able measure of emotional intelligence based on independent review. The EQ-i 2.0 has some distinct advantages over other emotional intelligence self-assessed measures due to being translated into many languages, a wide variety of norms and the availability of comprehensive 360 assessments (EQ 360 2.0), incorporating leadership comparisons.

Useful insights from others' perspectives into an individual's emotional intelligence can be gained from 360 assessments.

Social intelligence

Social intelligence is often simplistically referred to as 'people skills' as it is the ability to get along well with others and to get them to cooperate.

Social intelligence includes an awareness of situations and the social dynamics that govern them, and a knowledge of inter-action styles and strategies that can help a person to achieve their objectives in dealing with others. It also involves a certain amount of self-insight and a consciousness of one's own per-ceptions and reaction patterns.

Social intelligence is a combination of skills expressed through learned behaviour. By assessing the impact of your behaviour on others – the degree to which your dealings with them are successful – you can experiment with new behaviours and new interaction strategies.

Unfortunately, many people do not continue to learn and grow as they get older as they have developed a set of behavioural capabilities that have given them a degree of success. Some people never acquire the awareness and skills they need to suc-ceed in social, business or professional situations. Adults who lack insight and competence in dealing with others can make significant improvements in their work-related performance by understanding some basic concepts and assessing themselves against comprehensive models of interpersonal effectiveness.

The principles of social intelligence

Social intelligence consists of four key principles:

- Respect for others. People come from various walks of life, with cultural and educational backgrounds that are wholly unique. So, everyone has a different viewpoint or opinion. Each individual has feelings and thoughts and, as such, there should be an understanding that everyone deserves respect and consideration.

- Honour different perspectives. The what and why behind the perspectives of others must be understood. What is their belief and why do they hold this assumption? Every person is viewing the situation from a different perspective, as they each have their own experiences, skills, talents and insights.

- Having social intelligence does not necessarily require you to accept or understand an opposing viewpoint, but honours the fact that everyone is entitled to their own perspective.

- Behavioural awareness. Everyone has the right to feel whatever they choose to feel. However, there must also be awareness when automatic behaviour comes into play. This behaviour can be habitual and therefore not involve any forethought but is simply acted upon based on assumptions or ingrained beliefs. The ability to become aware of this automatic behaviour, however, enables these behaviours to be modified to achieve more desirable outcomes.

- Effective decision making. Social intelligence means comprehending that every aspect of life, including social situations, involves decision making. More importantly, every choice leads to consequences, both good and bad.

- In a team, decisions are made to lead or to follow, to cooperate or work independently, to contribute and get involved or stand and observe.

The SPACE formula of social intelligence

The SPACE formula describes a set of behaviours that make up social intelligence and social skills.

S – Situational awareness

People with good situational awareness are able to read cues within an environment and how events in it are playing out. This includes the effects on the emotions and behaviour of others involved. They may then be able to take steps to improve the atmosphere in an oppressive setting, or to maintain the mood in a positive one.

P – Presence

Presence describes the combined effect that a person has on others in a group due to their appearance, attitude, personality, body language and behaviour.

Through presence, opinions are formed of others and assumptions are made, which affects the way they are treated initially. In particular, distinctive physical and behavioural traits can have a major impact, especially if the opinions and assumptions made are false ones.

A – Authenticity

Authenticity is all about how true a person proves to be to the impression that they give, the attitudes they express and the expectations they raise with their promises or statements of intent.

Challenges to someone's personal beliefs and ideals, the conventions of their society, and the assumptions they make about themselves and others may question their underlying values.

This may require people to contrast their ideas and attitudes with their actual behaviour.

C – Clarity

Clarity is a measure of a person's capacity to articulate their thoughts, and to effectively communicate their ideas and their overall message in different social contexts. This aspect of social intelligence requires an individual to be both a good communicator and a good active listener.

E – Empathy

An integral part of social intelligence, as with emotional intelligence, is the ability to really understand another person's perspective, to see their point of view and to share in their reactions and feelings about a given situation.

How emotional and social intelligence are related

Professor Howard Gardner of Harvard University (1983) defined a theory of multiple intelligences, which introduces a practical approach to developing intelligences other than cognitive intelligence.

Emotional intelligence is one of Gardner's key intelligences. Some people have tried to stretch emotional intelligence theory to include skills involving people but, in practical terms, it makes more sense to think of emotional intelligence and social intelligence as two distinct dimensions of competence.

Social intelligence (Gardner's *inter*personal intelligence) is separate from, but complementary to emotional intelligence (Gardner's *intra*personal intelligence). Both models are needed in order to understand yourself and the way you interact with others. Some deficits in social intelligence arise from inadequate development of emotional intelligence; conversely, some deficits in social skills may lead to unsuccessful social experiences that may undermine a person's sense of self-worth, which is part of emotional intelligence.

Emotional intelligence and social intelligence can be considered as separate for purposes of discussion and analysis, but actually they are intimately interwoven.

The intelligence in empathy

Empathy is a fundamental component of both emotional intelligence and social intelligence, yet it is a highly misunderstood term. When people think of empathy, they often think first about sympathy and compassion. However, empathy is much broader in scope than simply feeling for or with someone. Empathy is about understanding things from the other person's perspective: what they see, feel and want, and truly trying to understand their situation.

Empathy involves deep active listening, which goes way beyond hearing and understanding the words being used. This is a very difficult skill to master.

Empathy is about being able to sense and read signals that people are sending in the course of an interaction. If you have good empathy you are able to read between the lines of dialogue and discern a person's motivations. Subtle but reliable signals, advertised in the face, eyes, posture and rhythms of speech, signify what people are really thinking about what you are talking about.

Your natural impulse will be to constantly try to bring attention and recognition back to yourself. By overcoming this, you begin to develop keen intuitive senses that support your ability to be empathetic.

The development of empathy

Empathy does not come naturally. You had to learn empathy by being taught it through the relationships that you had with your parents or carers and the manner in which they demonstrated empathetic behaviours.

Empathy is nurtured very early on in life. Nature gives the mother, through her physiological changes and the maternal instinct, the ability to support the child's empathetic development. Imitation helps to create the child–parent bond in the first few months. A very young child learns to recognise and show preference for its mother's voice and can understand and react to her emotional state. From this basis, you begin to recognise emotions in others and as this automatically signals your own emotional circuits, you copy what you see.

By having empathy you learn how to integrate into social groups – those of your family, friends and other people.

As a human being, you are a social animal. When you model empathetic behaviours others are more likely to adopt these behaviours themselves. These become quite an influential force in the regulation of emotions and in building relationships throughout life.

Empathy, the sensing of another person's feelings, allows for rapport. Empathy is an individual ability, one that resides inside each person. But rapport can only arise between people as it evolves and becomes more prominent through their interactions.

It is the obvious which is so difficult to see most of the time. People say 'It's as plain as the nose on your face.' But how much of the nose on your face can you see, unless someone holds a mirror up to you?

Isaac Asimov

Human factors

The term 'human factors' is not confined to one single area of scientific study but covers a range of diverse disciplines and is applied to systems that improve the efficiency of operation and the reduction of human error leading to accidents. The knowledge, concepts, models and theories are derived mainly from human science disciplines such as psychology, physiology, medicine, anthropometry and others.

None of the existing recognised disciplines can of themselves account for the full range of current knowledge about how and why humans function the way we do. As a result, the process of trying to consider human performance as a subject in its own right has necessitated a new term. The term generally used is 'human factors'.

Human factors is used to cover a broad number of functions that study people's performance in their work and non-work environments. It can mean many things to many people, and trying to understand all its implications can be daunting. Often the term is used following human error or critical incidents of some type and so it is easy to think of it negatively. However, human factors also includes all the positive aspects of human performance: the unique things human beings do well.

The primary focus of any human factors initiative is to improve safety and efficiency by reducing and managing human error. Human factors is about understanding humans – our behaviour and performance. Then, from an operational perspective, human factors knowledge is applied to optimise the fit between people and the systems in which they work in order to improve safety and performance.

Why considering human factors is useful

Everyone is working with greater uncertainty, ambiguity and change than ever before. Human factors helps employees and leaders to improve their effectiveness and sustain their efforts.

Developing a greater understanding of human factors won't stop bad or stressful things from happening, but can reduce the level of disruption caused by errors and the time taken to recover.

Human factors has been embraced by service industries where human error can lead to serious events that can result in the loss of life. These industries include aviation, heavy engineering, energy generation, oil and gas, and the health service.

The systems within these industries are dynamic: competing efficiency targets, financial pressures, high labour turnover and conflicting initiatives all create ideal preconditions for errors to occur at any time.

The last few decades have seen improvements and thus a reduction in critical events in a number of areas through assessments of human factors. This has been focused mainly around equipment and system reviews.

In analysing critical errors, the focus is more often on *what* happened instead of *why* it happened.

When human factors become useful

Human factors is useful in more complex system issues, such as the influence of culture, non-technical skills and the behaviours of senior staff. Creating a culture where behavioural change is put into practice through openness to learning and the willingness to acknowledge lessons learned is still far from being the norm in many organisations.

Consideration should be given to how human memory and attention mechanisms work, how humans process information from their environment and how human performance is influenced by environmental and situational factors, such as distractions and interruptions.

These are acknowledged, but often overlooked, in favour of more easily quantifiable and measurable systems, such as investigating and analysing incidents, conducting system reviews, developing root cause analysis tools, implementing safety management systems, and enhancing risk management and reporting systems.

The principles of emotional intelligence and social intelligence are the core components of the non-technical skills, the soft skills, involved in human factors, which is also the focus of this book.

Behaviour in business that drives the building of successful and powerful relationships is underpinned by:

- Situation awareness
- Team-based cooperation and coordination
- Decision making
- Communication

- Leadership
- Managing fatigue and stress

The benefits of human factors

Human factors:

- helps to retain a focus on what matters and supports effective behaviour

- uses situational awareness to help with anticipating varying circumstances by gathering information, recognising context and understanding intent

- improves planning and preparation to provide and maintain standards

- helps to identify and address barriers to communication

- improves communication by exchanging information clearly and concisely, acting assertively, empathetic listening, and coordinating with others

- reduces conflict and supports others

- helps to maintain objectivity and make authentic, quality decisions

- leads to better psychological wellbeing and health

- develops resilience – coping strategies and managing stress to maintain fitness for duty

- encourages team-based cooperation and coordination

- grows leadership capabilities, including coaching

A more focused approach on the non-technical skills in human factors considers recent advances in psychology, physiology and neuroscience and looking at how these can be applied to behaviour and to improve performance in the workplace. They are the cognitive, social and personal resource skills that complement technical skills, and contribute to safe and efficient task delivery.

Non-technical skills have not traditionally been a core part of the education system and curricula in apprenticeships, technical training, medical schools or academia. Rather they are expected to be picked up and learned on the job.

Human factors-based training focused around emotional and social intelligence skills, together with their practical application in the real world, can change this.

What are the non-technical skills of human factors?

The aim of human factors is to interface the best characteristics of people (behaviour, competencies, training) with the best characteristics of systems (equipment, procedures, processes) design and construction, maintenance, management and operation, with a view to eliminating or at least reducing errors in operation.

There are many books that cover ergonomics and the systems-based approach of human factors but very few that look at the non-technical aspects.

This book provides a practical handbook that covers many aspects of emotional and social intelligence involved in human factors that lead to developing successful and powerful relationships.

All I know is that I know nothing.

Socrates

Perception

You respond and make choices based not on absolute reality, but according to how you perceive the world. Everything you experience (your knowledge, understanding, involvement, exposure, memories, etc.) is a figment of your imagination. Although what you sense is accurate and truthful, your internal representation of it is not necessarily the physical reality of the outside world. Many experiences in daily life reflect the physical stimuli that send signals to your brain. However, the same neural circuitry that interprets inputs through your sensory organs, such as eyes and ears, is also responsible for your dreams, delusions and failings of memory. In other words, the real and the imagined share a physical source in the brain.

In order to make sense of the huge amount of information that bombards our senses, each and every moment, you unconsciously filter it. If you didn't do this, your brain would become overloaded so that even the simplest tasks would be impossible to perform.

Perception depends on complex functions of the nervous system, but subjectively seems mostly effortless because this processing happens outside conscious awareness. This internal representation is all you know. By the time you become aware of information coming through from the world around you it has been filtered.

The world you perceive is not reality – it's a filtered representation of reality.

Sensory input

All perception involves signals in the nervous system, which in turn result from physical or chemical stimulation of the sense organs. As human beings, we experience an external event through our sensory input channels. They help us to assess situations, analyse events and interpret our surroundings.

The traditional view is that there are five main senses:

- Visual: what we see – pictures, use of colour and decoration, a preference for information presented graphically and pictorially
- Auditory: what we hear – sounds, voices, music, being able to process information presented verbally
- Kinaesthetic: what we feel – a preference for touch and to experience things personally, to learn well by trying and doing
- Olfactory: what we smell (aroma) – linked strongly to mood and memories because smell goes directly to the limbic system faster than the other senses
- Gustatory: what we taste – responses linked to food and drink

There are a number of other sensory input channels beyond the traditional five that most people are familiar with – these include abilities to sense hot and cold, to sense pressure, feeling thirsty and hungry, coordination (motion, equilibrium and spatial orientation through the vestibular system) and perceptions about time. About 20 discrete sensory inputs have been identified.

The illusion of attention

The things you pay attention to create your moment-to-moment perception of reality. Everything else is lost or blurred. Not only do you see only what you are focused on, over time you can be so accustomed to familiar environments and circumstances that everything blends into the background.

You believe with confidence that your eyes capture everything before them and your memories are recorded versions of those captured images. However, only the illuminated portions that you spotlight with your attention appear in your perception. You ignore the periphery of your attention or think about something else.

In 2010 Professor Daniel Simons asked participants to watch a video of a basketball being passed around between several people, with a particular focus on the basketball itself. When the experiment was over, Simons found that many participants were so focused on watching the basketball being passed around that they failed to notice a man in a gorilla suit gesticulating in front of the camera.

The change within the video wasn't subtle; the gorilla was very obviously in the middle of the frame and for a number of seconds. Simons concluded that participants were experiencing inattentional blindness: failing to notice a major change because they were so focused on another task. In this case, because participants were asked to focus on the movement of the basketball, their brains prioritised that task in order to do it properly, thereby missing the other things happening in the video.

They engaged in what's referred to as attentional selection, which is when a person selects certain things to focus on in order to achieve a task and filters out anything that is unrelated to that objective. You have to focus your attention on something in order to be able to see it. Seeing isn't the same as looking. What you see and what you think you see have a lot of consequences for your daily life.

You know when you are aware of something unexpected, but you are not aware of the times that you have missed something unexpected. The problem with inattentional blindness is not that it happens so often, it's that you don't believe it happens. Your tendency to believe you have perfect perception and recall leads to mistakes in judgement in your mind and in the mind of others.

Change blindness

Change blindness is a perceptual phenomenon that occurs when a change in a visual stimulus is introduced and the observer does not notice it. With change blindness, you don't notice when things around you are altered to be drastically different from what they were a moment ago. Magicians build careers around perceptual blindness to conceal changes in your visual field.

An inability to recognise every change in a complicated situation is generally attributed to your brain's capacity to remember complex images in a broad scope with focus on, mainly, the larger aspects without recognising smaller changes.

Your visual intelligence can only detect changes in those parts of a situation on which you are focused. Your inability to detect changes in those areas where attention is not focused is thought to reflect fundamental limitations of human attention. In general, this is because your brain cannot possibly process every element of an experience and has to prioritise what it believes to be important.

Do you construct detailed representations of the visual world in those areas that you do not pay attention to? This question is as yet unanswered, but is the subject of current research.

Change blindness has become a highly researched topic and may have important practical implications in areas such as eye-witness accounts and distractions while driving.

Filters

The perceptual systems of the brain enable you to see the world as stable, even though your sensory information is typically incomplete and rapidly varying. Before you make an internal representation of an event, data is filtered through your internal processing filters.

Everybody filters information that they receive from the real world. The filters transform what you experience with your senses into your internal thoughts. They clarify your experiences and help to give them meaning. These internal processing filters sift information received through your senses to create your own unique perspective. They can work positively and negatively.

There are three processes by which you create the filters to give your individual model of the world:

- Deletion
- Distortion
- Generalisation

Using the three filters you create your own model of the world, which implies that your experience is always slightly separated from reality. Your model of the world will be different from some-one else's model (Figure 2).

Figure 2 How you develop a coherent representation of reality

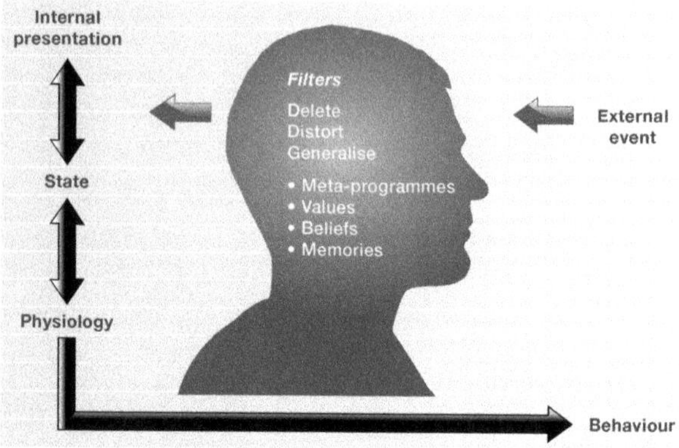

Deletion

Deletion involves removing the bulk of information from the environment around you and internally so that you are not consciously aware of your breathing, heart rate, digestive processes, etc. every moment of the day and night. The brain and nervous system can't keep up with the total amount of information received and so your experience is edited for simplicity. It has been found that your conscious mind can only handle four bits of information at any one time and that the rest is ignored or deleted. You are forced to omit certain aspects of your current experience by selectively paying attention to other aspects of it. In other words, you focus on what is apparently most important at a specific moment in time and the rest is deleted from your conscious awareness. Sometimes you overlook things that would help you if you noticed them.

Because of deletion, your perception can change dramatically as you are missing bits of information about your experience as it goes through your sensory filtering.

The unconscious mind takes in a lot more information than you are consciously aware of. Information deleted from the conscious mind may be stored somewhere in the memory system by the unconscious mind to be retrieved in some way, if appropriate.

Distortion

Distortion involves changing the reality of a situation through creatively imagining what it could be. The external environment is changed into something else. Examples of distorting a situation are through visualisation, dreaming or hallucination.

Being intimidated by certain people, frightened of a harmless situation, procrastinating or misinterpreting what someone says are examples of how you distort reality.

When you fantasise or dream, you are using the distortion filter. To plan the future, you distort time with the prediction of actions. No one knows what the future will be, so experiences from the past are used and information is shifted through sensory filtering in order to work out how you think the future will be.

A number of cognitive biases have been identified that distort your view of the world:

- Confirmation bias: more attention is paid to evidence that supports your beliefs and plays down or ignores evidence that doesn't.
- The bandwagon effect: you are more likely to do something or believe something when many people are doing or believing the same thing.
- Illusion of control: you believe that you have some level of control or influence over certain outcomes, even when you haven't.

- The halo effect: if you like one quality or trait about a person, company, brand or object, you tend to view their other qualities or traits more favourably.

Generalisation

Generalisation is how you unconsciously generate rules, beliefs and principles about what is true or untrue, possible or impossible. You do this by taking a few examples and then creating a general principle.

The process of all your learning and drawing of conclusions so that information can be applied for the achievement of any task requires generalising.

Learning occurs so that you don't have to relearn every time you use a new pen, open a door, put on a different article of clothing and so on. Knowing how to do something to a satisfactory standard (e.g. driving a car) takes time and practice so that these behaviours become habitual and unconscious.

Generalisations are the mechanisms that generate beliefs and are the basis of stereotyping and prejudice.

Beliefs, memories and values

Your beliefs, memories, values and experiences affect how you perceive and interpret current events and challenges. They can have emotions attached to them that can also have an influence on how you work with them.

Beliefs

These include things you trust as being true and what you believe you can or cannot do. Beliefs can be positive, creating success, or be negative and limit your behaviour. Beliefs are formed in many unconscious ways, are influenced by parents, teachers and friends, and so on. You can also be affected by other people's negative beliefs or preconceptions of what they think you can or cannot do.

Beliefs help you to make sense of the world around you and can either empower you to achieve success or limit your thinking about getting ahead. The only way to change your beliefs, prejudices and faulty perceptions is through changes in your perception.

Memories

These are more likely to stick if they combine information and emotion, and can form the basis of your reaction to current situations that will influence your present and future. New experiences can bring back old memories and emotions, so that you react to the old memory and emotion rather than experiencing the current situation. This can lead unconsciously to a negative response.

Values

Values are like an evaluation filter, interpreting what is important to you and what makes you feel good. Values drive your behaviour and can either motivate or demotivate. Values also affect your choice of friends, hobbies, interests and how you spend your time. Examples of values include accuracy, perfection, efficiency, financial security, support and openness.

Memory

The traditional, and prevailing, view of memory is that it works like a warehouse of files on a computer's hard drive. Within this view, your brain records an accurate and complete record of events. If you have trouble remembering, it is because you can't find or get access to the right file, or because the hard drive has been corrupted in some way. However, it is difficult to explain how people have memories that are both clear and vivid while also being wrong. Yet this happens, and it is not infrequent.

Memory distortions occur in everyone's life. In critical situations, the various people involved go back and forth over what happened, and you are sure that you remember both what you and what the others said. In constructing your memory, however, there is what you said, but there is also what you communicated, what the other participants in the process interpreted as your message, and finally, what they recall about those interpretations. Emotions will also change your perception of the occasion.

It's quite a chain, and so people often strongly disagree in their recollection of events.

Psychologists recognise that while you have a good memory for the general gist of events, you have a bad one for the details. Furthermore, when pushed for any unremembered details, even well-intentioned people making a sincere effort to be accurate will inadvertently and unconsciously fill in the details by making things up, employing their expectations, desires, prior knowledge and beliefs. To exacerbate this, people firmly believe the memories they make up.

Therefore, it is important to be aware that the details of scenes and incidents you remember, though they seem very real, are often biased.

Yours is not the only truth

Every person has a different view of reality. They will notice things that you have missed and vice versa. Their view of reality is as valid to them as yours is to you.

People who believe that everyone experiences the world in the same way that they do set themselves up for misunderstandings, just as people who believe that others should see the world as they do are setting themselves up to be constantly disappointed.

People's actions make sense from their reality, which we can never fully know or understand. Their choices make sense to them. Often their behaviour or actions don't make sense or appear wrong when judged from your perspective.

Even if people intellectually recognise that their reality is not the absolute truth, and that others have a different reality, they can still create problems if they believe or insist that their view is the right one or the only one that everyone should have.

State, physiology and behaviour

A state refers to a condition of mind or feeling. A state may simply be an emotion, but it usually refers to a more multichannel experience – a gestalt of the neurological processes (mind and body) within an individual at any given time.

Emotions come and emotions go, but moods seem to remain for a longer period of time. While emotions tend to be fleeting, lasting for seconds or perhaps minutes, moods tend to last for hours and, sometimes, days. Moods could be described as medium-term background feelings that set a context for short-term emotions.

Each emotion sparks a distinctive physiological reaction, the body's program for dealing with the different situations that arise in your emotional life. Happiness signals the brain to suppress worries or negative thought processes and increases the body's energy level.

Your primitive survival mechanism responds to anything that you perceive as danger by triggering the fight or flight survival response. Modern life readily induces this response, which can lead to stress. Every human has a habitual response to stress that is either learned or genetically implanted.

The physiological responses include:

- Increased heart rate and blood pressure. This pumps blood around the body to get oxygen and sugars to the cells that you will need for fight or flight.

- Rapid breathing to make more oxygen available throughout the body.

- Adrenaline, also called epinephrine, is released by the adrenal glands. This hormone helps to maintain increased heart rates and informs the liver to release stored sugar to provide energy.

- Muscles that you use to fight or flee tense.

- Blood is directed towards the brain and major muscles and away from the skin surface, digestive organs and reproductive organs.

- Senses are heightened for survival vigilance.

- Perspiration occurs to cool down the body's increased metabolism.

Prolonged tension in one or more of these systems can lead to stress, with accompanying symptoms and associated health issues.

Your behavioural responses to your emotions and physiological reactions are driven by your emotional and social intelligence.

The way the brain works

Neuroscience is the scientific study of the nervous system and covers many disciplines. As human beings, we are complex organisms, with our brain connected to intricate neural circuits and biological systems. The nervous system is the most complex organ system in the body, with most of the complexity residing in the brain.

At its simplest level, cognitive and behavioural neuroscience looks at how the workings of the brain address complex questions about its interactions with the environment.

Neuroscience addresses what is happening in our brains around how we think about experiences and interactions with others. Understanding how we create thoughts, and how brain and neural pathways develop, can provide insights to explain how we deal with certain situations, consciously and unconsciously.

Learning how to change habits and rewire our thinking can be a valuable tool to creating greater flexibility and new approaches to challenging situations.

Thinking

Your brain has a powerful ability to put together and make sense of whatever is put before it.

Neural networks in your brain behave as a self-organising system that encourages incoming information to organise itself into stable patterns in order for you to make sense of the world. This patterning behaviour is the basis of your perception. Your attention will attribute relevance and meaning when your existing patterns are triggered.

The thinking and language systems that we have developed are good at logic but poor at perception, which gives rise to some inadequacies and dangers in our current thinking.

Language is our main instrument of communication and thinking. The excellence of language as a descriptive medium has made it relatively crude as a device for perception. Because we can describe complex situations, we have not needed to enrich our patterns of perception through language.

Language creates mutually exclusive categories, such as right and wrong, good and bad, friend and enemy, and so on. This allows the logic of contradiction. However, the logic of perception has been overlooked until recently.

Principle, logic and argument form the basis for much of your thinking. Where it breaks down is in your assumption that your perceptions and your values are common and universal.

The way that critical thinking has become considered to be the highest form of thinking has some unfortunate consequences. This traditional way of thinking is based around what is held to be true and what can only be checked by logic and argument. A high proportion of politicians and those in the legal and medical professions are only accustomed to this way of thinking. The result is a strong tendency towards disagreeing and attacking. When they have low levels of emotional and social intelligence, such that the person or their character is criticised rather than the belief, this behaviour can be interpreted as argumentative and disrespectful.

Critical thinking lacks the productive, generative, creative and design elements of lateral thinking that are often needed to tackle problems and find a way forward.

According to Dr Edward de Bono, the leading authority in the field of creative thinking, every valuable creative idea must always be logical in hindsight. If this wasn't the case, the value of the idea couldn't be recognised. It would only seem like a crazy idea. It is now known that an idea obvious in hindsight may be invisible in foresight.

Humour helps us to understand perception better as it gives direct insight into changes in perception, followed by changes in emotion. This is something that cannot be achieved by logic.

Empathy

Empathy is an inborn quality *and* is a skill you learn through the way that your parents or carers modelled empathetic behaviours.

Empathy is nurtured very early on in life, particularly in regard to the relationship you had with your mother or primary caregiver. Your mental representation of the world was formed through that early relationship and it became quite an influential force in the development of your empathic behaviour and the way that you regulate emotions.

The maternal instinct is inborn and innate. Relationships through attachment suggest that nature gives the mother through her physiological changes the ability to support the child's empathetic development.

Imitation helps to create the child–parent bond in the first few months. A very young child shows preference for its mother's voice and can understand and react to her emotional state. Through this, you learned to perceive an emotion in the faces of others by the way that the emotion automatically signalled your own emotional circuits. You began to recognise emotions in others and copied what you saw. Imitation becomes a complex, subtle and often unconscious process – an automatic part of your social functioning.

The purpose of imitation is to understand the emotional states of others and to understand what they are going through, feeling, sensing – which is vital for knowing how to interact with them. This learned empathy is a continuous, automatic process.

As humans, we are wired to connect as we are social animals. Empathy helps you to integrate into social groups – those of your family, friends and other people that you have to connect with.

The neuroscience of empathy

Empathy is an individual ability, one that resides inside the person. When you model empathetic behaviours it means that others are more likely to adopt these behaviours themselves. Empathy allows for rapport. However, rapport can only arise between people and emerges through their interactions. Two (or more) independent brains don't necessarily react consciously or unconsciously to each other but the individual minds become, in a sense, fused into a single system.

The system of brain interconnectedness relies upon specific neural circuitry and related endocrine systems, which inspire others to engage with you.

Your brain contains neurons that are important in empathy by helping to create an instant sense of shared experience:

- Mirror neurons, which mirror and mimic what another person does and feels
- Oscillators, which coordinate you physically with another person by regulating when and how your body moves to be in tune with another – an unconscious feeling of resonance
- Spindle cells, which are involved in your intuition and rapidly assess your judgements and beliefs about whether to trust the other person, in conjunction with other intuitive measures

This interface of minds is a stabilising mechanism outside of both of you and emerges as you interact. The way that it works means that you cannot be emotionally stable on your own – it's not that you should or shouldn't be stable on your own, but without this stabilising effect of the interface you can't be.

The deep consequence is that through the sum total of our interactions we create each other.

Persuasion, kind, unassuming persuasion should be adapted to influence the conduct of men.

Abraham Lincoln

Communication

Communication occurs when information is channelled by a sender or transmitter to a receiver via some medium.

The receiver decodes the message and gives the sender (transmitter) feedback.

There are multiple parts to effective communication that rely on all of the components working effectively. Communication is not just transmitting a message (by saying something or sending an email), it involves ensuring that the message is accurately passed on, received *and* understood.

For successful communication to occur the transmitter (sender) of the message and the receiver need to know that the message has been conveyed and understood correctly.

This is easily achieved by including a feedback loop whereby the receiver indicates to the transmitter that the message has been received and correctly understood.

Breakdown in communication

Breakdown in communication occurs when there is interference in either transmission or feedback (or both). This can be language, filtering, selective perception or emotion.

A communication breakdown occurs when a message is incomprehensible to one party or is entirely absent between two people. Although some communication breakdowns are intentional, most of what we say is unconscious and from poor habits learned from others.

Interference is the main cause of any breakdown in communication and can occur due to:

- The message being transmitted too loudly
- The message being transmitted too quietly
- Background noise
- Language
- Cultural differences
- Stereotyping
- Stress
- Anger or other intense emotion
- Confusion
- Illness

The only way that you can know if your message has been received as sent, is to notice what the response is. If the response is not what you expected from the message sent, then it has been received differently and you've communicated something other than you intended. It's your responsibility to change how you are sending the message until you get the response that tells you that your message has been received and correctly understood.

Non-verbal communication

When communicating face to face, a lot of information is transmitted non-verbally.

Non-verbal communication forms the context against which the listener evaluates the meaning of the words used and your sincerity. While the words convey messages about whatever you are talking about, the non-verbal communication around them is conveying messages about your relationship with the listener and how you feel about what you are saying.

So, all the time, your facial expressions and other body language (posture, gestures, etc.) as well as your voice tone are sending messages that are open to interpretation, whether consciously or unconsciously. Voice tone and facial expressions or body language can modify the meaning of what you say.

Non-verbal communication includes:

- Posture and body movement
- Size and number of gestures
- Facial expressions
- Eye contact
- Tone of voice
- Volume of speech
- Pace of speech
- Listening

Interpretations are used to form guesses about how you are feeling, what you are thinking, your intentions and what you are likely to do next.

This can make telephone calls, messages transmitted using mobile technology and email more challenging as many non-verbal channels of communication are lost, which can lead to misunderstandings.

Incongruence

It is important to be aware that whatever you do, or don't do, you are always communicating.

The meaning of your communication depends as much on the context as on what you are saying or not saying – on how you are expressing yourself through your use of words and your body language.

Incongruence occurs when your words, tone and body language all say different things. For the receiver of your message, or listener, this creates a state of cognitive dissonance – that is, they receive conflicting signals and are unsure about which message to believe.

As body language is judged to be a more reliable mode of communication, incongruent body language suggests that your words can't be trusted. This is because underlying emotions are difficult to control and fully suppress and these are expressed through body language – especially as micro-expressions on the face.

Incongruent gestures can also be what are called *ambivalent signals*. This is where there is no intention to deceive but by saying one thing while your body language suggests another means that you are presenting conflicting information to an audience, which can end up confusing them. Gestures and words that don't match one another can lead to a breakdown in communication.

When you use and read non-verbal communications correctly, you communicate well.

Metaphors and association

Metaphors and associations are conceived from experience and applied to the being and doing of the life you know. A metaphor transfers meaning in imaginative and creative terms, from one object to another through association.

A metaphor is a figure of speech that describes a subject by associating with, comparing it to and describing it in terms of another, otherwise, unrelated topic. Metaphors include similes, parables, analogies, parallels, literary metaphors and so on.

The association is often important in one or two dynamic ways that have deep, significant meaning to the person using the metaphor.

Paying attention and working with metaphors may enhance the results you get from communication because:

- metaphors can represent experience more fully than abstract concepts and so enable more effective communication
- metaphors condense information, making things more tangible and easier to work with
- the metaphor for an experience has a similar structure to the experience that it represents
- metaphors provide an important route into the deeper, more profound levels of a person's thinking
- when people experience change, both the metaphor and real-life experience generally change in tandem.

As a human being, you appear to be hardwired to think in metaphors and you are also hardwired to respond to metaphors through storytelling, anecdotes and so on.

Rapport

To influence or persuade another person to change their mind or to behave in a different manner, you need to start from where they are. You need to start to understand how they are seeing and perceiving the situation around them. What may be important to you may not matter to them. If they don't think the message is relevant to what they feel is important they will not be interested.

When people feel that their viewpoint is under attack, they dig in, harden their attitude and resist. This is particularly true if they are unaware of how your viewpoint differs from theirs and are not given good reason to see things differently. The very existence of their reality is under threat and their primary objective will be not to change their mind.

To get the person into rapport with you is all about removing obstacles to communication, taking things at a pace that works for them, and using verbal and body language that they find appealing and makes sense to them. This gives them the chance to start finding their way from where they are to where you would like them to be.

If resistance is encountered through lack of rapport, the first thing to do is to pay more attention.

It does not mean giving up your viewpoint and accepting theirs as true – it just means respecting their reality and working with it.

Poor listening skills

Listening is a core component of empathy and building rapport. You need not possess a psychologist's listening aptitude to develop listening skills. If you don't possess a natural aptitude for listening, you have to work at developing the skill.

You are going to be less effective at listening if you:

- carry out other tasks or concentrate on something else while the other person is talking
- are thinking of how to respond rather than tuning into the speaker
- are listening out for comments that will act as an introduction to what you want to say
- interrupt or talk over the speaker
- get ahead of the conversation and finish the speaker's sentences
- are looking for opportunities to add witty comments, stories and opinions at the expense of the other person's story
- focus more on facts than on feelings
- are obsessed with details, so that you miss the point of what the speaker is trying to say
- forget about what was talked about previously
- are not in control of any nervous or uptight body language signals
- hint at any disapproval or impatience with your tone and body language.

Who doesn't occasionally trespass across these boundaries of poor listening?

Tight schedules, demanding goals and people that try your patience can combine to take you away from listening effectively.

Working on listening more effectively is a start to becoming more emotionally and socially intelligent.

Good listening skills

Everybody likes to be listened to and understood. It affirms and validates us as human beings.

People who provide you with opportunities to be heard and the time to listen to you are rewarded with your trust and loyalty.

To develop key listening skills:

· Face the speaker and maintain eye contact

· Be attentive, but relaxed

· Keep an open mind – listen without any judgement

· Be curious about what you are hearing

· Listen to the words and try to picture what the speaker is saying

· Don't try to come up with any solutions

· Wait for the speaker to pause and then ask clarifying questions

· Ask questions only to ensure understanding

· Try to feel what the speaker is feeling

· Give the speaker encouragement to continue and reflect back the speaker's feelings ('you must be really pleased', 'I can see that you must be confused')

· Check your understanding by summarising what you have heard

· Pay attention to what isn't said – to non-verbal cues

Effective listening requires deliberate effort and a keen mind. Effective listening promotes good relationships, provides a flow of new ideas and information, keeps you updated with regard to any changes and implementations, encourages participation and ensures that situations don't turn into crises.

Barriers to communication

Communication can be more difficult when it occurs across professional, specialty or hierarchical barriers. You often don't use the same technical language, jargon, acronyms, or have the same level of understanding or awareness of others' roles.

Indecisive leaders

Leaders who are indecisive or those who lack confidence may be reluctant to communicate as a way to avoid showing vulnerability. This silent approach to leadership can lead to distrust in the work environment, and may lead to informal gossip taking over as the main communication channel.

Egotistical leaders

These leaders have a distorted image of their own importance. They put their own agenda, status and gratification ahead of others by their thoughts and actions. They blame others when things go wrong as they believe they are always right, cannot be taught anything and do not admit mistakes. Communication becomes limited. Employees are driven by fear of threats and punishments, which leads to decision making being deferred to the leader. They do not question instructions, won't raise concerns and will withhold information – especially any communication that is deemed negative.

Narcissistic leaders

Narcissistic leaders are preoccupied with themselves and how good they look. They find people who they cannot dominate too difficult to manage. They won't accept responsibility and blame everyone else as they are mainly concerned with looking good. They thrive on making everything into a great drama so that they can respond to the challenge with their sheer brilliance.

Conflict

Communication can cause conflict: it's a way to express conflict and it's a way to either resolve it or perpetuate it. Very often a breakdown in communication, or interpretation of that communication, will inflame or facilitate a conflict situation.

Conflict is a natural occurrence and is inevitable as you see things in different ways to other people or have a different point of view. In the workplace, when multiple employees work together, their varying backgrounds and opinions often lead to different conclusions or ideas on how to handle work projects.

Employees who are unhappy or uncomfortable in their workplace are less likely to communicate openly. A major problem exists when colleagues or work team members don't get along.

By learning how to resolve conflict in a professional, respectful manner, you can reduce tension and strengthen relationships. The skills learned enable you to work better together by knowing how to navigate disagreements. Instead of fighting, insulting or ignoring one another, you can learn how to listen to each other and to collaborate. This helps you to take a more thorough look at any situation and consider other possible solutions.

Your conflict resolution skills can increase your efficiency by resolving problems quickly and effectively without getting too many people involved. This allows the flow of activity to continue in the workplace without extended disruptions due to any unresolved issues.

Teaching these skills in the workplace encourages a deeper understanding of situations that arise. Good conflict management allows you to move beyond your own emotions and opinions to make objective decisions. You learn how your colleagues feel and think, as well as how to interact with them better.

The role of empathy in conflict

The most important emotional and social competence necessary for resolving conflict is empathy – the process of identifying emotionally with another person. In fact, empathy is the foundation of all conflict management.

Empathy is certainly a skill demonstrated by those who keep themselves disentangled from conflict.

Within conflict scenarios, it can be difficult to force yourself to view and feel events the same way that another person does. Neither you nor the other party is wrong for seeing events differently; perception and response are functions of different core personalities and social interaction styles.

A large percentage of conflicts are rooted in these types of core personality and social interaction style perceptions. Personality plays a substantial role in the amount of conflict we experience with co-workers, employers and clients.

If you hope to resolve conflicts, your first step is empathically identifying with the other person's viewpoint and for them to empathise with yours. Once this step is taken, defences are brought down, and it becomes easier for you both to be willing to meet halfway.

Workplace relations can be improved by:

- tactfully confronting tensions based around different social interaction styles
- establishing compromises that consider the social interaction styles.

The only way to change someone's mind is to connect with them from the heart.

Rasheed Ogunlaru

Behaviour

Social interaction styles

Both emotional and social intelligence are underpinned by self-awareness.

Social interaction styles consider your preferred pattern of behaviour for a large number of situations. Your interaction style represents itself through your daily interactions and is not subject to judgement or evaluation – it is merely your acquired preference.

At a surface level, your style is closely linked to whether you tend to assert yourself or respond to others in social settings, and whether you tend to display emotion or secure control in group settings. It shows itself in your communication style, conflict-management style, the job roles you are drawn to, and the way you perceive yourself and your contributions in the workplace.

The underlying model of social interaction styles involves two primary dimensions: how assertion is expressed and how emotions are managed.

Assertiveness

You may prefer to take the lead in assertive ways, speaking directly and frankly while focusing on strategic objectives. Alternatively, you may prefer to respond to input from others, and sharing your own ideas as a way to build upon others'.

Emotional control

You may prefer to express yourself outwardly in social settings or to maintain composure and control.

The two extremes of the assertive and emotional variables provide four basic combinations that can be thought of as behavioural preferences across a range of situations (Figure 3). Some people blend these four patterns almost equally, while others may tend to prefer one behavioural pattern over others.

Figure 3 Social interactive styles based upon assertiveness and degree of emotional control

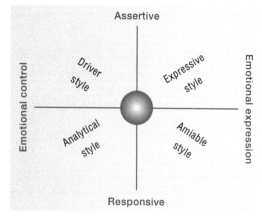

Years of research into workplace success have shown that you have one of four social interactional styles. Each style has its own preferred way of acting, thinking and making decisions.

Understanding these preferences allows you to determine the best way to interact with anyone.

- Driver style: people control their emotions and speak assertively. They prefer to be decisive and control a situation. Their focus is on outcomes and results. They are not concerned about relationships or feelings and may come across as blunt at times.

- Expressive style: people show their emotions readily and speak openly. They are optimistic and creative and enjoy sharing their ideas. They may appear to others as unfocused and easily distracted.

- Amiable style: people show their emotions openly and prefer to ask questions rather than give orders. Relationships, feelings and personal security are important to them. As they want the time to consider the impact of decisions on everyone, they may appear hesitant at times.

- Analytical style: people control their emotions but tend to ask questions rather than give orders. They are focused on logic and accuracy, and they act deliberately to achieve that end. At times, their focus on getting things perfect may be perceived as being critical.

Focus and pace

The expressive and amiable styles display emotions openly and respond best to those who do the same. Their focus in achieving an outcome is through *relationships*. As their tendency is to readily show emotion, this helps them to build relationships at work, but it can have mixed effects on team cohesiveness.

The driver and analytical styles tend to view displays of emotion as not necessarily being relevant in the workplace. These styles are more focused on the *task* itself. Both of these styles care about personal relationships and feelings but consider these to be relevant only in certain settings, preferring to express themselves more rationally at work.

The expressive and driver styles will put more energy into situations and what they are trying to achieve, and operate at a faster pace.

The analytical and amiable styles have a tendency to conserve their energy and, as a consequence, are more deliberate in the way in which they go about things, and so are slower paced.

The circle in Figures 3-10 shows where emotionally intelligent and socially intelligent engagements take place. Here, the focus and pace of the interaction is more in harmony with others involved and can be adapted easily to take account of their responses.

Driver style

Driver-style people have the strength of will to work well under pressure, and are always ready to take on responsibility.

They have a clear idea of their ambitions and goals, as well as the directness and forcefulness to achieve those goals. It also means that they will tend to have a competitive attitude, and will generally follow their own ideas rather than work cooperatively with others.

The driver style is often a useful trait in a manager or leader, especially in situations where there's a need for decisive action and clear direction. Note that this certainly doesn't mean that someone with a driver style will be an effective leader – that depends to a huge degree on the situation – but the core features of this style tend to match well with the challenges of leadership.

You will have difficulty with the driver style if you:

- Waste their time
- Are unclear and use too many words of explanation
- Get too personal or try to chat too much
- Are disorganised
- Stray from the purpose of the meeting
- Ask irrelevant questions
- Make wild claims
- Try to control the meeting

You should aim to:

- Get down to business quickly
- Be specific in questioning
- Use time efficiently
- Provide alternatives for them to choose from
- Be factual and to the point
- Talk about results and outcomes
- Avoid too much detail
- When finished – go!

The characteristics of the driver style

- Manner: confident and controlling. They can have a confrontational and abrupt manner. They may frequently interrupt. Make efforts to control outcomes. Direct action.
- Facial expressions: limited and controlled.

- Eye contact: long duration and direct. Their gaze is fixed and intense.
- Body movement: upright, thrusting posture. Short, sharp gestures that are frequent and confined to drive home the points they are making.
- Voice: loud, clear, quick, clipped and determined. The conversational flow is pushing towards getting things done quickly and effectively.
- Motivation: power and authority.
- Basic fear: failure.
- Valued words:
  - Results
  - Highly competitive
  - Customised solution
  - Research
  - Innovative
  - Unique
  - Efficient
  - Expedient
- Stress response: autocratic – tells others what to do.

Expressive style

Expressive-style people are at their most comfortable in a social situation and interact with others in open and expressive ways.

They are active in their approach and orientated towards other people. This is the root of their socially confident and unreserved attitude. They thrive on the attention and approval of other people and are more motivated by praise and appreciation than most other styles. Despite their outgoing attitude, they're often unwilling to risk causing offence and they'll often avoid possible confrontations.

The expressive style will be at their most motivated surrounded by other people and with the scope to communicate freely.

You will have difficulty with the expressive style if you:

- Socialise too much
- Control the meeting and keep strictly to a structure
- Are impatient or controlled
- Input too much detail
- Take away their freedom to choose then close down the conversation
- Patronise or remain determined that your way is the only way

You should aim to:

- Expect some element of socialising
- Talk about opinions and other people
- Give your ideas about the product/service
- Be enthusiastic and energetic
- Be fast paced
- Offer incentives

The characteristics of the expressive style

- Manner: enthusiastic, free-flowing, playful and animated. They use humour and laugh easily. They can be impatient and finish others' sentences for them. Make efforts to be involved. Act impulsively.
- Facial expressions: expressive and warm.
- Eye contact: flighty and dancing. Their gaze is frequent.
- Body movement: animated with expression. Frequent, open gestures that are large and expansive.

- Voice: loud, fast and modulating. The conversational flow is flexible and random.
- Motivation: public praise and recognition.
- Basic fear: rejection.
- Valued words:
  - Quick
  - Cutting edge
  - Easy
  - Competitive
  - Innovative
  - Possibilities
  - Fun
  - Flexible
  - Big/huge (adjectives about potential)
  - Opportunity
- Stress response: attacks – verbally confrontational.

Amiable style

Amiable-style people will tend to be far less open or direct. They are more inclined to respond to events, rather than take proactive steps themselves.

They have a concern for other people, combined with a reluctance to take direct action. They are consistent and reliable in their approach, preferring to operate in situations that follow established patterns, and to avoid unplanned developments. Because of this, people with the amiable style tend to be quite resistant to change, and will take time to adapt to new situations.

They are patient, reliable and consistent. They have the capacity to apply themselves to work, focusing on what needs to be done in a productive way. They can relate to, and appreciate openness, honesty and sincerity to other people and provide support or help others. Their understanding and patient approach means that they are good team workers through offering assistance and guidance in resolving problems of a personal nature.

You will have difficulty with the amiable style if you:

· Get straight to the point
· Keep the discussion focused all the time
· Keep offering opinions or increase the complexity of the discussion
· Cause them to respond quickly
· Dominate or control the discussion
· Are rapid or abrupt
· Make wild claims
· Are extremely factual

You should aim to:

· Be friendly, and show interest in them personally
· Have some social chat before getting down to business
· Take time to ask open questions
· Be informal and non-threatening
· Include guarantees and be reassuring wherever possible
· Give your presentation a personal touch

The characteristics of the amiable style

· Manner: friendly, calm and relaxed. Considerate and sincere. They easily mirror others' mannerisms. They typically allow others to take the lead. Make efforts to build relationships. Act supportively.
· Facial expressions: smiling, warm and varied.

- Eye contact: soft and caring. Their gaze is sincere, intermittent and empathetic.
- Body movement: an approachable, relaxed posture. Frequent nods of agreement. Infrequent gestures but open and flowing.
- Voice: softly spoken, slow and modulating. The conversational flow is responsive, respectful and cooperative.
- Motivation: security.
- Basic fear: insecurity.
- Valued words:
  - We/let's
  - Commitment
  - Concern
  - Security
  - Sensitivity
  - Step by step
  - Teamwork
  - Long term
- Stress response: acquiesces – appears to give in.

Analytical style

Analytical-style people are concerned with working within the rules. They are concerned with accuracy, structure and understanding the ways things work.

They like to have a clear idea of what they are doing and what is expected of them, so they are far more motivated in situations that are clearly regulated and planned. In general, the analytical style are not independent by nature, preferring not to be left to make decisions or take actions without having done a full analysis and taking care of the all specifics.

The natural focus of the analytical style is on details, facts and figures, and they tend to be at their best when they have time to organise and plan their work. Their affinity for questions of accuracy and regulation means that their style tends to suit situations where high standards and quality needs to be considered.

You will have difficulty with this style if you:

- Are disorganised and casual
- Are late
- Provide personal incentives
- Push or gently persuade
- Use testimonials or opinions
- Are flippant or use methods that try to increase the appeal around what is being discussed

You should aim to:

- Be well prepared
- Get straight down to business
- Listen carefully
- Be specific and logical
- Be persistent and thorough in questioning
- Be formal and unemotional when challenging
- Give them time to give their point of view

The characteristics of the analytical style

- Manner: punctual, deliberate and meticulous. Diplomatic. Reserved and nervous. Ask lots of questions. Make efforts to establish process. Act cautiously.
- Facial expressions: limited, unemotional and not very expressive.

- Eye contact: intense, serious and questioning. Their gaze is limited and reflective, occurring when answering questions.
- Body movement: upright, rigid and formal posture with limited movement. Small, infrequent gestures that are confined.
- Voice: quiet, slow, measured and monotonal. The conversational flow is deliberate, precise and intensely focused. Their speech is hesitant to ensure the correct choice of words.
- Motivation: standard operating procedures.
- Basic fear: conflict.
- Valued words:
  - Caution
  - Logical
  - Research
  - Analysis
  - Projections
  - Thorough
  - Proof
  - High standard
- Stress response: avoids – withdraws from the situation.

Tensions between the styles

There will be tensions between the styles. Each style has a unique set of priorities and preferences as to whether the relationship or the task aspect of a situation is more important; and each has its own pace in terms of how fast things should be done.

The driver and expressive styles tend to prefer a faster pace while the amiable and analytical styles both tend to prefer a slower pace. These style combinations will get along well as far as pace is concerned, but watch out for their priorities!

The driver and expressive styles are both relatively fast paced. Yet the expressive style places more emphasis on people than on tasks, while the driver style tends to pursue goals with less concern for relationships or feelings. Some degree of tension is likely to result in their interaction due to their differences in priority.

The amiable and expressive styles place more emphasis on relationships than tasks. Yet the expressive style places more emphasis on doing things more decisively and quickly, while the amiable style tends to pursue relationships or feelings in a more considered way and will prefer to take their time doing so. Some degree of tension is likely to result in their interaction due to their differences in priority.

There will be much more opportunity for tension between the analytical and expressive styles due to differences both in pace and focus!

Reactions to pressure

The right level of tension produces the highest level of productivity. However, your reaction to increased pressure will be affected by factors both inside and outside your work. Your way of responding will be influenced by how you have coped with similar situations in the past and how successful you were in managing your stress and anxiety at that time. It will also be influenced by your personality and your social interaction style.

Each social interaction style possesses predictable behaviours when faced with stress and highly pressurised situations. Each style behaves in an exaggerated form of that style when under stress that appears rigid and extreme. This is a strategy to try to release tension.

The driver and expressive styles display fight behaviours, driven by their preference around assertiveness. The driver style will become autocratic and tell people what they want them to do, while the expressive style will attack in a verbal confrontation.

The amiable and analytical styles will display flight behaviours, driven by their preference around responsiveness. The amiable style will acquiesce to demands, while the analytical style will avoid confrontation, avoid people and avoid making decisions (Figure 4).

Figure 4 How each style responds to stress

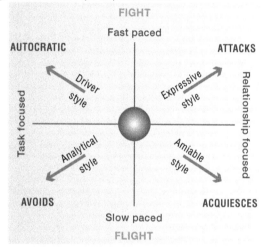

There are radically different responses to stress. By understanding these responses, you will know exactly what to expect and are more likely to incisively diffuse any tension.

Driver style conflict responses

In conflict situations, driver-style people are likely to:

- Take a direct, aggressive approach
- Rapidly escalate the level of confrontation

- Become competitive and create win/lose outcomes if there is a lack of cooperation
- Attempt to clear the air immediately
- Solve problems with more regard for closure than feelings
- Listen to creative input to solve problems

Because of their tendency for frankness, driver-style people will tackle conflict directly. Some people appreciate their straightforwardness; others find it offensive. They are not afraid of hurting people's feelings if they feel the resolution is right and are often heard saying, 'They'll get over it!' in regard to emotional responses.

Because of their intense desire for closure, however, they will listen to creative input that solves the issue and will quickly move to resolve issues rather than harbour any resentment.

In conflict scenarios with the driver style, you should:

- Avoid arguments
- Listen to their complaints and ideas for resolution
- Ask for the best ways to solve the conflict
- Own up quickly to any mistakes made (don't try to make up excuses)
- Be ready to put the situation behind you and move forward

Expressive style conflict responses

In conflict situations, expressive-style people are likely to:

- Avoid the scene when they sense negativity
- Try to dismiss or smooth over the situation (adopt a superficial approach)
- Become emotional and offensive – take criticism or conflicts personally

- Seek control or revenge by persuading others to side with them
- Openly joke about or trivialise the conflict (but be internally upset)
- Overwhelm their opponent with a monologue

Expressive-style people are quite uncomfortable in confronting conflicts as this goes against their friendly, people-orientated nature. They are good at getting people to see their side of the argument and rally them to their cause, trying to win by virtue of a majority. They are also inclined to use superficial fixes by making light of the situation, restoring an air of amicability. They avoid people whose tone communicates anger, frustration or impatience. Criticism is often taken as a threat to their image, and they may respond by attacking the opponent or venting their frustrations. They may also act as if the problem is solved (in the hope that it will pass) when there is still an undercurrent of conflict.

In conflict scenarios with expressive-style people, you should:

- Approach them in a friendly and positive fashion
- Use self-deprecating humour to ease tension
- Look at a collaborative approach to the conflict instead of taking sides
- Ask for their thoughts and ideas for resolution and listen without interruption

Amiable style conflict responses

In conflict situations, amiable-style people are likely to:

- Avoid interpersonal aggression
- Become quiet

- Freeze up and may flush with frustration
- Become emotional and/or defensive
- Express frustration and feelings to people other than the offending party
- Give in or fake agreement to avoid losing approval

Recognising the signs of escalating conflict or frustration with amiable-style people is important. They are often subtle in their methods of disagreement and, as a result, they are either overlooked, or attempts are made to superficially placate them.

Conflict builds when they begin to stop talking and/or flush, display a lost or bewildered look, or respond in a defensive manner.

In conflict scenarios with amiable-style people, you should:

- Enquire about their thoughts and feelings regarding the situation
- Demonstrate concern and respect with good listening skills
- Outline the necessary steps in resolving the conflict

Analytical style conflict responses

In conflict situations, analytical-style people are likely to:

- Increase resistance and shift into passive-aggressive behaviour
- Overpower others with facts and logic
- Become defensive
- Withhold information
- Respond with 'what if..?' questions and 'prove it' statements
- Judge their opponent and the situation in distinct factual terms

Resolving a conflict with analytical-style people is going to require a thorough resolution. They examine all the events that led to the conflict, then carefully lay out the groundwork to prevent this scenario from recurring. They will not readily change their views without overwhelming evidence. Their initial response in conflict will be defensiveness, and they will quickly attempt to prove that they are right. They may withhold any necessary input for solving the conflict or even refuse to participate at all in the resolution process.

In conflict scenarios with analytical-style people, you should:

- Avoid forcing or pushing for a resolution (adopt a patient approach and move slowly and cautiously)
- Avoid debate and blaming
- Ask for their analysis of the situation and for their input to prevent future conflict from occurring
- Take notes

Increasing pressure

What's even more interesting is what happens if this exaggerated style – this backup behaviour – doesn't appear to be working. When the stress doesn't go away, it makes sense to try something else.

Each style will move in a predictable pattern through the other styles of backup behaviours. Of course, the behaviour expressed is not well developed as this is not natural behaviour for that style. In itself, the expression of behaviour in this way will add to the burden of stress.

Each style manages their emotion in a certain manner. In the next phase, they maintain the way in which they regulate their emotions but, as their attempts at influencing and changing the situation have not been that successful, they alter the way that they assert themselves.

The driver and analytical styles both keep their emotions under control and so the next attempt to influence the situation maintains this control and keeps their emotions in check, but uses their assertiveness differently. The driver style will go into *flight* mode and avoid, while the analytical style will go into *fight* mode and become autocratic.

The expressive and amiable styles both freely express their emotions in an attempt to build relationships. They continue to show and use emotion and, again, will try an alternative approach by changing their assertiveness. The amiable style will go into *fight* mode and attack, while the expressive style goes into *flight* mode and acquiesces (Figure 5).

While the changes in behaviour provide a short-term release of tension, they are unlikely to result in an effective outcome.

As the changes in assertiveness have not proved successful, the next stage is to return to using assertion in the way that feels most comfortable and to change the way that emotions are managed and expressed.

Of course, these ways in which emotions are used in social situations, with their normal level of assertion, are not well developed for any of the styles, so the manner of emotional expression and the accompanying behaviours is likely to be unpleasant.

Figure 5 Responses to increased stress – changes in assertion

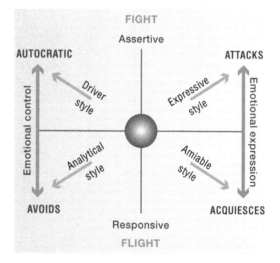

The driver and analytical styles both return to their usual assertive ways but start expressing and showing their emotion. The driver style will go back into *fight* mode and attack, while the analytical style will go back into *flight* mode and acquiesce.

The expressive and amiable styles both return to their usual ways of assertion but will begin keeping their emotions more in check to start feeling more in control. They become less concerned about the relationship. The amiable style will go into *flight* mode and avoid, while the expressive style will go into *fight* mode and become autocratic (Figure 6).

Figure 6 Responses to further stress – changes in the way emotions are expressed

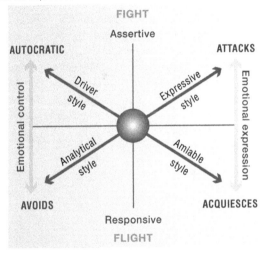

Expressing emotion in a way that does not come naturally combined with a familiar manner of assertion may help on occasions but, if these behavioural changes have not had the intended impact, all the styles move into the final backup stage. In this stage, the final resort, the person believes that the only option left open to them is to keep using emotions in this unnatural way *and* to attempt the alternative approach to their assertion. The resulting behaviours will be expressed in a very ugly fashion and will be completely out of character. In these situations, assertion will spill over into aggression – very severe passive aggression or very severe aggression.

This is the point when relationship tension becomes so intense that interpersonal connections begin to unravel and communication becomes even more difficult; relationships become unproductive, untenable or worse. The driver and analytical styles both continue expressing and showing their emotion but change their assertive approach.

The driver style will reduce their assertion in *flight* mode and avoid, while the analytical style will increase their assertion in *fight* mode and attack. The expressive and amiable styles both control their emotional responses keeping them in check but change their assertive approach. They believe that the relationship is beyond redemption. The amiable style will remain in *fight* mode, raise their assertion and become autocratic, while the expressive style remains in *flight* mode, lowers their assertion and will attack (Figure 7).

Figure 7 The final resort to increased stress – changes in assertion and emotional expression

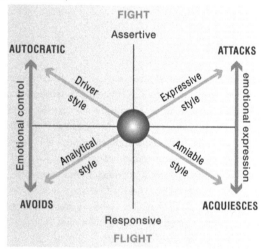

Stress responses of the social interaction styles

As pressure increases and becomes more extreme, each social interaction style moves in a predictable pattern through the other styles of backup behaviours.

The first-stage backup is an extreme, rigid form of the main social interaction style.

The second-stage backup involves maintaining the management of emotions in a familiar manner but changing the level of assertion.

The third-stage backup involves changing the expression of emotion to work with them in an alternative way and attempting to use assertion in familiar ways.

The final-stage backup involves keeping the change of working with emotion *and* changing the expression of assertiveness.

The stress response of the driver style is:
autocratic–avoid–attack–acquiesce.

The stress response of the expressive style is:
attack–acquiesce–autocratic–avoid.

The stress response of the amiable style is:
acquiesce–attack–avoid–autocratic.

The stress response of the analytical style is:
avoid–autocratic–acquiesce–attack.

The behaviours are not natural for each style in the various stages of backup and each expression of behaviour will manifest in each stage differently within each style.

When you look below the surface of people's actions and reactions, you will see deep-seated patterns around behavioural preferences and social interaction styles. Learning to recognise these behavioural responses will give you a great deal of influence and control in understanding these situations.

The stress response of the driver style

Driver-style people are focused on results and the outcomes of a task. They want to achieve what they set out to do quickly and fear failure. These are very strong drivers for the driver style. They readily display *fight* behaviours driven by their preference around assertiveness. They will become autocratic easily and tell people what they want them to do. This is often perceived by the other styles as bluntness, especially when they are pressurised and annoyed.

The response through the remaining backup behaviours happens very quickly in the first instance. As there is little variation in pace, it may not be very obvious. It can often occur within a few sentences.

If they are unable to get the outcomes that they want, they will try to change the subject (avoid). Further pressure provokes an attack, which can be personal and is focused directly at the person pushing them. For example, 'You are making me very angry.' Finally, they will give into requests (acquiesce): 'All right, we'll do it your way.'

They do not bear grudges, so pushing them through the pattern is unlikely to change the relationship focus (which is fairly minimal anyway). However, they can easily lose their respect of others whom they consider to be weak and ineffective.

The next stage of backup behaviour seen is avoidance behaviour where they can avoid any direct issues by providing facts and data to support their position, and/or avoid managers and people who they see being the cause of the issues.

Often problems that arise are around relationships and so in an attempt to work with their emotions and the emotions of others, they can attack people for wanting to bring emotion into the situation.

This causes further problems and may lead to the final stage of the stress response. Driver-style people can acquiesce to pressures and demands (Figure 8) by changing job role, moving to another department or resigning.

Figure 8 The stress response of the driver style

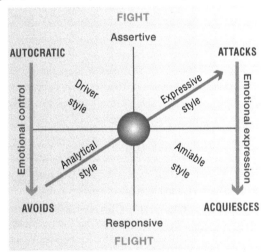

The stress response of the expressive style

Expressive-style people like people who give them praise and recognition for who they are and the support they give. They like to get involved and don't like to be excluded or rejected. They are verbally astute and generally good at communicating their opinions and ideas. Under pressure, they will attack others. Often they will use humour to diffuse tension and are good at making people laugh about others' idiosyncrasies. Further pressure can lead to them using sarcasm. Using their energy and verbal shrewdness, they often take up a cause for the team, arguing on their behalf.

They want to keep relationships intact, as far as possible. As they don't really want the person pressurising them to reject them, the next stage is to go along with what they are being told to do – albeit reluctantly. They will do what they are instructed as quickly as possible with little attention to detail and quality.

The next stage is to stand up to the person causing them issues. They will be autocratic, telling the person what they think, what they expect them to do and how they expect them to do it. They will stand their ground and become very argumentative and demanding. If the issue persists, they will completely avoid the person causing them problems. They will have nothing further to do with the individual and will work unceasingly to completely undermine that person at every opportunity.

Remember, they are excellent communicators and are good at building relationships through networking, so they will have lots of contacts throughout the organisation. They have the ability to convince anyone who engages with them how much of a problem they are facing, why this is such an issue and who exactly is responsible for this. If you have caused them to go into avoidance (Figure 9), you are best advised to look for another job!

Figure 9 The stress response of the expressive style

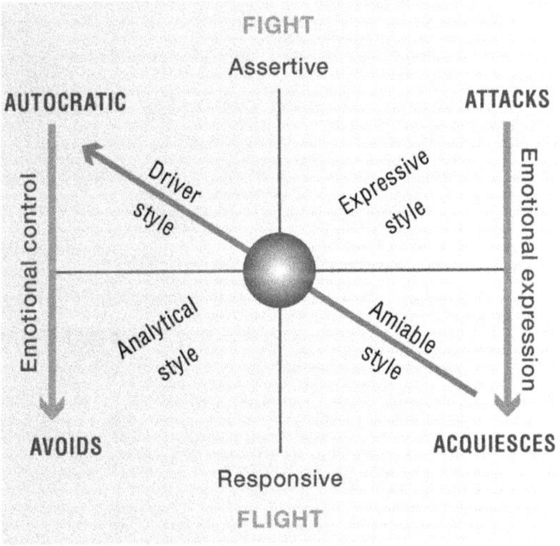

The stress response of the amiable style

Amiable-style people like to feel secure in their relationships, in the team and in their role. They are kind, friendly, good natured people, always willing to help and expect the same of other people. They are disappointed when others don't share these values. They don't like any situation that makes them feel insecure. Stress, in any form, leads to some feelings of insecurity.

Under pressure, they will acquiesce to demands. They may not like this behaviour in themselves but it provides an immediate release of tension. They may privately berate themselves for not having stood up for themselves and for not refusing the demand. They will seek comfort in others by talking this through.

As demands and pressure increases, they go on to attack. However, they will not directly attack any person responsible for their stress for fear that it may destroy the, already fragile, relationship. They will attack in a passive-aggressive manner that involves procrastination, sullenness and verbal attacks when the person(s) involved is not around to hear them.

Further pressure leads to avoidance tactics. Bottling up and controlling emotion leads to stress-related health issues. So, avoidance behaviours include time off sick, extended leaves of absence and being signed off through stress.

If stress continues at work, they will confront the person involved in an extremely autocratic fashion, highlighting all the times the issues arose with very specific detail about the demands, the dates and times, why it caused problems, how it made them feel and so on (Figure 10).

Figure 10 The stress response of the amiable style

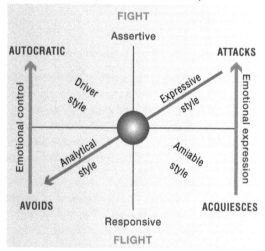

Often this completely out-of-character, uncontrolled outburst is so intense that it may lead people to say things that they later regret.

This stress pattern is not good news as people can end up taking out grievance procedures or on a disciplinary as a result of their behaviours.

The stress response of the analytical style

Analytical-style people like to complete their tasks in a logical, procedural fashion. They like to pay attention to detail and will ensure that they have all the facts and data that they need. They have very high standards for themselves – they are perfectionists – and expect the same of others. They dislike conflict but can be perceived as quite critical of others if they are not given all the information that they want.

If they are asked to do something that makes them feel uncomfortable – either through lack of resources or, what they think are, unreasonable demands – their reaction in the first instance is to avoid making any commitment. Emails will remain unanswered or telephone calls not returned or they will deliberately overlook bringing up the issue.

Once they have checked all the facts and have all the correct data, they will appear autocratic as they assert themselves armed with precise information. Sometimes their first avoidance might go unnoticed and, only when they show signs of unrelenting tensions, will they become autocratic. Often, they can oscillate back and forth between these two stages for quite some time before attempting another approach.

They will take a long time to get to the final two stages. As they dislike conflict, they will acquiesce under increasing pressure. This is not done with good grace and will be an emotional display in a dramatic manner ensuring the person involved is well aware of their displeasure.

The final stage will not be obvious as they appear to go back into their typical avoidance behaviour *but* they will attack to get even (Figure 11). This will be extreme passive-aggressive behaviours that involve sabotage. Examples include withholding information, deliberately missing deadlines, letting someone's tyres down, malicious and snide remarks on social media using a pseudonym and so on.

Figure 11 The stress response of the analytical style

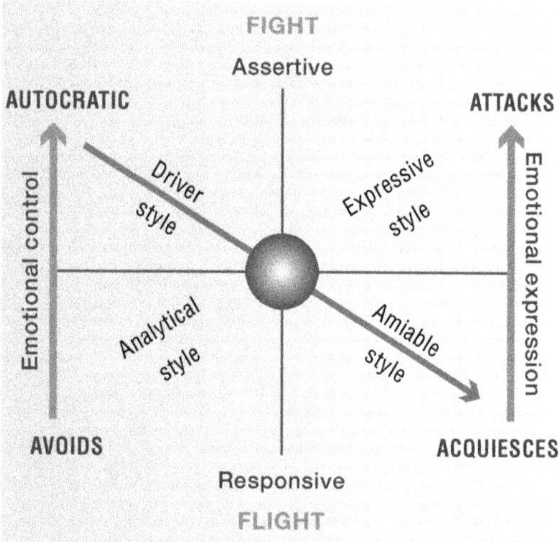

Ideal behaviours for ideal interactions

It would be unreasonable to expect everyone in your workplace to adjust to all of the idiosyncrasies and characteristics of your personality and social interaction style. Those with patterns similar to yours will be more comfortable with your natural communication and management style. With these people, few compromises are necessary and you can just be yourself.

Diplomacy, restraint and compromise enter in most often when you are dealing with people of opposing styles. If you refuse to compromise when dealing with them, you will be met with equally powerful forces of resistance and resentment leading to conflict.

It is reasonable to expect that, if you are willing to adapt your own preferences, then other people – sensing a step in their direction – will alter their response and reaction to you.

Understanding and changing your behaviour towards others is not about being manipulative. It is about aiming to convey clearly your true intentions by validating the other person and empowering them to become more authentic in their interactions and relationship with you.

A reasonable expectation is to negotiate compromise first by demonstrating compromise:

- Set a business-like helpful tone
- Engage in appropriate levels of sociability
- Aim benefits at the needs of the other person
- Expect high receptivity and candour
- Be factual
- Analyse and answer
- Voice strong convictions

Developing emotional and social skills

The emotionally and socially intelligent professional recognises that each person has an idiosyncratic comfort zone and that there will be issues when those zones of comfort are violated. With such recognition comes opportunity. The opportunities are for you to demonstrate that you understand other people's specific needs for security and to demonstrate your own flexibility to meet them at their point of comfort.

Emotional and social intelligence develops through experience with people and learning from success and failure in social settings. It takes a lot of effort and hard work.

To become emotionally and socially intelligent, effort should be applied in these areas:

- Begin by paying more attention to the social world around you
- Practise mindfulness
- Study social situations
- Be more aware of your own behaviour
- Be more aware of emotions – yours and others
- Explore and gain an understanding of different perspectives
- Become more adept at flexing your behaviour
- Work on becoming a better communicator with more diverse groups
- Communicate authentically
- Be assertive in compassionate ways that express what you are feeling or wanting without appearing aggressive
- Accept your limitations around who you are and what you know
- Understand how your judgements and prejudices affect your thinking
- Work on becoming a more effective listener
- Regain a childlike wonder and curiosity about everything that you experience
- Develop your coaching capabilities

Organisational culture

Within certain organisations and teams there exists a definite hierarchy. There is a power gradient; the leader at the pinnacle coordinates, directs and makes all the decisions. If the hierarchical gradient is too steep, with a number of layers, the leader has a massive position of power.

However, this power is not absolute. Confident leaders have an accurate perception of their talents; they know their strengths and their weaknesses and will readily admit them. This is good leadership and more leaders like this are needed.

Issues can arise through the personality and behaviours of the leader and how they use their emotional and social intelligence. Employees who don't find their managers approachable may not seek help or offer input when need arises.

Arrogant leaders have a distorted perception of their skills and talents. They may be fairly competent and good at what they do. They don't like to be challenged, even if they claim that they do. They are led by their ego, which may be due to confidence or esteem issues and usually cover up this self-doubt with bravado.

People working within a hierarchy need to feel that they can raise concerns or question decisions. This must be understood by everyone at all levels within the chain of command. It is important that people learn how to raise concerns in suitable ways.

One way to reduce the hierarchy is for the leader to build their coaching skills, to invite responses and ask about thoughts and concerns in appropriate ways. This builds a more diplomatic environment.

Organisational structure

An organisation is not a fixed entity. It is an ongoing event – an interconnected web of interactions in which everyone plays a role.

The culture within the organisation is simply the result of the interaction among the employees working together over a period of time. Culture can have an impact on communication and relationships.

Effective communication is essential for a positive, healthy culture in the workplace. Transparency in communication is required at all levels for better understanding of work and better bonding among individuals. Leaders and managers clearly pass on necessary information to all employees so that they know what they actually are supposed to do. The employees are very clear about their key responsibility areas in order to deliver good outcomes and perform at their best. Roles and responsibilities are delegated according to specialisation, educational qualification and area of expertise.

Employees have the liberty to share their ideas and concepts on an open forum in order to find innovative solutions benefiting all.

Some organisations encourage or require diverse work teams, but don't offer informal and formal ways for employees to build rapport. This lack of rapport can cause tension, which can lead employees to avoid interaction or to completely disengage, which can include extended leaves of absence.

Behavioural and personality assessments

Behaviour and personality can be assessed using a variety of well-researched, reliable and valid psychometrics. The market for these assessments is very competitive. There is a wide assortment of different products available (well over 10,000). Some are based on similar principles and are branded in a variety of ways.

Many are based around the social interaction style model. Some label the styles using different nomenclature – as elements of nature, as animals, as birds, as colours and so on. Some are more sophisticated and go into more depth than others.

Organisations initiate training and development programmes to develop their people based on principles of emotional and social intelligence, and often, a psychometric assessment other than social interaction styles may be incorporated into the programme.

There are other psychometrics that can give very valuable insights into human behaviour in social circumstances. They include DiSC, Myers Briggs Type Indicator (Steps I and II) and instruments based on the Big Five (Openness, Conscientiousness, Extraversion, Acceptableness and Neuroticism). These are more complex and are more difficult to pragmatically apply within training programmes. Some involve complex models, terminology and applicability in the workplace that limit their long-term retention value by ordinary people. The level of support in their application with training programmes can also be very variable.

Most good psychometrics can be used and explored in many ways and dimensions to gain a real understanding of the insights highlighted. Valuable pragmatic knowledge around self-awareness and awareness of others can be embedded into the very fabric and culture of the organisation. To do this really effectively requires the use of the psychometrics over many years.

Often, however, there appears to be a desire to try out the next, new, shiny personality assessment. This often happens through a lack of understanding of the psychometrics used when managers have only been superficially exposed to it; they feel they know it and want something different.

Emotional and social intelligence in organisations

There are a lot of companies offering emotional and social intelligence development as part of leadership and management programmes. Sometimes, these include training around human factors. It is often the case that these are modules bolted on rather than being fundamentally integrated into the programmes.

There is also a prevailing attitude that one- or two-day workshops will give people the necessary skills to become more situationally aware and more emotionally and socially intelligent.

Many organisations' cultures are not conducive to implementing learning and allowing people to develop long-term, sustainable change due to pressures around delivering for the short term.

People receiving training on emotional and social intelligence competencies and capabilities in human factors return to their work environment full of enthusiasm, but the behavioural change quickly disappears. The reason why this occurs is that the person's behaviour was expected to change without changing anything else.

The organisation wants the training programme to improve the situation but doesn't want it to change anything in the way that they have been operating the situation.

Long-term sustainable change can take place. Development targets outputs, rather than inputs. It requires diagnostic assessment whereby the unique issues and opportunities facing the organisation are explored, and aspects of the culture, leadership, operational processes and human resource thinking is challenged and understood. Any proposed change requires full commitment at the highest levels within an organisation. This commitment devotes the necessary time and resources to making any agreed changes happen. This does not mean purely a superficial verbal arrangement but a basic and seismic shift in observable attitude and behaviour that supports everyone's efforts to make embeddable change succeed.

Employee engagement

Employee engagement is a property of the relationship between an organisation and its employees.

A fully engaged employee is one who is fully absorbed by their work and enthusiastic about the environment in which they work. This drives them to take positive action to further the organisation's reputation and interests.

Good employee engagement is supported by:

- Perceptions of the ethos and values of the organisation
- Effective internal employee communications
- Treating everybody with respect
- Employee perceptions of job importance
- Employee clarity of job expectations
- Career advancement and improvement opportunities
- Regular feedback and dialogue with superiors
- Quality of working relationships with peers, superiors and subordinates

Developing people really is the key to having an engaged workforce and achieving business success.

People feel valued for their contribution and they understand that the organisation supports them to be the best that they can be. Done efficiently, good engagement provides the means to motivate and involve people through authentic interactions.

A healthy organisational culture, supporting good engagement, encourages the right focus around behaviour to create the best environment to build successful and powerful relationships. Progress occurs at the individual level, the level of the team and at the organisational level.

People work with good emotional intelligence and social intelligence capabilities developing the core components of the non-technical skills – the soft skills – involved in human factors. Disruptions and the time taken to recover from errors are reduced, productivity improves and profitability increases.

Reading list

Bar-On, R. (1997). 'Bar-On Emotional Quotient Inventory: A measure of emotional intelligence'. Academic paper found in *The Bar-On Emotional Quotient Inventory (EQ-i): Technical manual*. Toronto, Canada: Multi-Health Systems.

Bar-On, R. (2004). 'The Bar-On Emotional Quotient Inventory (EQ-i): Rationale, description and psychometric properties'. Academic paper found in G. Geher (Ed.), *Measuring Emotional Intelligence: Common ground and controversy*. Hauppauge, NY: Nova Science.

Boyatzis R.E. and Goleman D. (2007). *Emotional Competency Inventory*. Boston: The Hay Group.

Chabris, C. and Simons, D. (2010). *The Invisible Gorilla: And other ways our intuition deceives us*. HarperCollins.

De Bono, E. (1995). 'Serious Creativity'. *The Journal for Quality and Participation*, 18, 12–18.

De Bono, E. (2000). *Six Thinking Hats*. Penguin.

Gardner, H. (1983). *Frames of Mind: The Theory of Multiple Intelligences*. New York: Basic Books Inc.

Goleman, D. (1995). *Emotional Intelligence: Why it can matter more than IQ*. New York: Bantam.

Goleman, D. (1998). *Working with Emotional Intelligence*. New York: Bantam.

Goleman, D. (2006). *Social Intelligence: The new science of human relationships*. New York: Bantam.

Mayer, J.D. and Salovey, P. (1993). 'The Intelligence of Emotional Intelligence'. *Intelligence*, 17, 433–442.

Mayer, J.D., Salovey, P. and Caruso, D.R. (2002). *Mayer-Salovey-Caruso Emotional Intelligence Test (MSCEIT) user's manual*. Toronto, Ontario, Canada: Multi-Health Systems.

Salovey, P. and Mayer, J.D. (1989). 'Emotional intelligence'. *Imagination, Cognition, and Personality*. 9 (3): 185–211.

About the author

Robin Hills has over 35 years' business and commercial experience helping executives and leaders develop business performance through increased self-awareness and understanding of others.

Robin is Director of Ei4Change – Emotional Intelligence 4 Change – a company specialising in training, coaching and personal development focused around emotional intelligence, positive psychology and neuroscience. Ei4Change's Advanced Emotional Intelligence Programme and Master Practitioner in Emotional Intelligence Programme are endorsed by the ILM.

Robin focuses on supporting personality and behaviour in business. His clients include small start-up companies through to large multinational corporates, the public sector (including the NHS) and charities.

His style, as a facilitative, consultative leader, is to encourage people to take responsibility and to get involved in a range of practical, business-focused, yet fun, training activities that aid and encourage learning on a one-to-one or group basis.

He is registered and accredited with the British Psychology Society as a Test User: Occupational Ability and Personality

(Level A and B) and uses a range of internationally recognised profiling tools to assess type, trait, behaviour and emotional intelligence. He is a Member (Business) of the Association of Business Psychologists and sits on the North West Committee.

Through his work in emotional intelligence, Robin researches techniques that support coaching interventions and experiential methodologies to support cathartic conversations within the work environment.

Based upon this work, Robin has spoken and delivered key-note speeches and workshops at international emotional intelligence conferences. These have been held in South Africa, India, the Middle East, the United States (Harvard University) and the United Kingdom (the University of Manchester and the University of London).

His educational programmes on resilience and emotional intelligence are used in educational establishments in South Africa and India and he is teaching over 8,000 students in 135 countries through online emotional intelligence programmes.

Robin manages monthly meetings in central Manchester that provide innovative thinking and interactive, evidence-based learning enabling people to reach their full potential and develop their skills so that these are relevant and up to date.

Contact details:

Email – robin@ei4change.com
Website – www.ei4change.com
Address – 17 Crown Gardens, Edgworth, Bolton BL7 0QZ
Telephone – +44 (0)161 244 8884

CPSIA information can be obtained
at www.ICGtesting.com
Printed in the USA
LVHW012207100721
692283LV00009B/519

9 781912 300082